YES,
THERE ARE STUPID QUESTIONS

Yes, There Are Stupid Questions

How to Believe in Yourself and Attack Your Dreams

Rob Fisher

Palmetto Publishing Group
Charleston, SC

Yes, There Are Stupid Questions

First Edition

Printed in the United States

Library of Congress Control Number: 2020912633

ISBN-13: 978-1-64111-867-5
ISBN-10: 1-64111-867-9

Jake,

If you struggle with writing, you don't know what you believe. You think you lack the gift, but you're unsure of your ideas. Get your thoughts to the point of certainty, and you can write anything. It's taking what's in your mind and saying it—nothing else.

—R. F.

Contents

Introduction

Welcome.

Yes, There Are Stupid Questions is my first book in a series called *Off the Chest*. I answer ten subconscious questions people ask when attacking a dream and offer unique advice that avoids generic personal-growth chatter.

I've kept things short for your benefit and have refused to mirror the industry norm. I have no pointless content that fills pages and zero regurgitated fluff typically found in the self-help genre. *Yes, There Are Stupid Questions* defies the genre's copycat persona by standing proudly in its brevity, and refusing to linger. My goal is to encourage a quick read that gets you out into the world and away from my book. I can't guarantee you'll leave inspired, but I promise you'll have the tools.

By day, I'm a technical and opposition scout in international soccer, and I'm presently building a nonprofit that focuses on scouting overlooked players in the global youth market.

Enjoy *Yes, There Are Stupid Questions*, and don't be afraid to throw it in a backpack or pair it with a glass of Bourbon.

In a quest to achieve our dreams, we ask stupid questions. These are a few.

Give It

It's not about playing guitar
It's about writing music
It's not about singing
It's about having a voice
It's not about pride
It's about standing tall
It's not about soul
It's about showing passion
It's not about toughness
It's about having guts
It's not about your head
But your heart
It's the reason somebody goes right instead of left
Takes a step forward or a step back

Lead, inspire, be creative
Live with purpose
Sunshine and chocolate get old
Rainbows fade
Vacations are basic
Traveling is not
The world needs your talent—give it.

CHAPTER 1

Can I Rebound?

I'm talking about life, not basketball. We ask this with every defeat, and the answer is yes.

To start, what you want is the same as what you need. The idea of life dragging you on some journey of wisdom for the sake of circling back to the realization that it's about what you need, and not what you want, is nonsense. The Rolling Stones have a song called "You Can't Always Get What You Want," and you should skip it every time.

When you strike out going for your dream, don't start believing that quitting is an act of maturity or that you should stop and do something "safe." The worst thing you can do is think that wanting a dream is something you grow out of. What you want is what you need, and what you need is what you want. Go after it, keep your head up, and never stop.

Let nobody convince you that life is about the word "can't." If you want to change the world, you can. If you want to do something great, you can. Big or small, dreams hide when you don't believe in them.

Stay stubborn, and never lose confidence. It's the most unattractive thing you could ever do, losing your confidence. You know how a dog looks when it hears something and stands up straight? Do that as a human. No matter what your dream is, know that it's real, and it's possible.

Can you rebound? Can you rebound from the first strikeout? Can you still have what you *want*, despite life knocking you down? You can. I'll tell you a story:

> I met a guy at a concert. He said he'd won his ticket by being "caller 5" on a radio station.
>
> He said to me, drunkenly, "Want to know the secret to winning?"

"Go on," I said.

"Just never hang up."

I said, "I don't think that's a secret."

"What do you mean?" he said.

"Isn't that life? Just never hanging up?"

I think he got it.

If you want something bad enough, there's a way. If you stick with it and you're creative and willing to work, you can beat anything life throws at you. You deserve what you want, so walk tall, and believe in who you are. There's no secret to hanging tough and you can rebound from the worst of it. We often act weaker than we think, but we are tougher than we know. Your head will psych you out, but you and your heart are capable of anything. Your soul will always be bigger than life's hand. Remember that, and you'll rise.

CHAPTER 2

Can God Help?

Deep breath. Religion has never been my medicine, so I'll give you some thoughts.

1. Believing in something is positive, as long as it's not a crutch. If you're in a burning building, trust your brain.

2. If you worship a god that puts you on your knees, stand tall afterword. Never expect what forces you down to pull you up.

3. Let's talk about "church." I'm not convinced most people know why they go. They go

because they want to feel grounded and to be with a community that believes in humility. A humbled feeling that centers them and reminds them who they are: a human being—nothing more, nothing less. It restores belief in their size and reels them back to the middle.

Where the problem comes in (and I speak about Christianity) is when things are said in unison like, "He will come again in glory to judge the living and the dead, and his kingdom will have no end." What was once a community gathering of fair reflection is now religion. When you follow something you can't see, while being told you're judged—both now and when you die—when you never asked to be born in the first place, you're existing in fear.

These prayers and creeds are intimidating yet are followed by messages of positivity that rope you in. They say, "God loves you," for example. Well it should; it made you, according to religion. "God has a plan" and "Christ died for us" are others. By mixing fear with love, religion makes it impossible to refute and tough to abandon. It suppresses you while reassuring you. It locks you in chains while holding the key. You recite something negative, but the following sermon is positive.

By attending church, you're looking for a chance to exhale and for a boat to sit in with others. When it becomes a place of judgment, confession, and salvation for the faithful, you're no longer a community of liberators, but you are individuals in servitude. Hypocrisy defines religion, and church is the instigator.

4. When things work "in your favor," so to speak, know that your actions are the cause, not your prayers. Some call it luck; some think that "everything happens for a reason," but you're allowed to see it logically. When positive change goes your way, it's you looking differently at the past and moving forward. Luck, and all its relatives, aren't related to divine intervention, karma, or prayer. If you think your good fortune was some higher being manipulating life for your personal gain, then you're egotistical.

You're not that special. You can squint your eyes, fold your hands and bow your head, but change happens with you. Nothing is controlling you getting or you not getting what you want.

When two people shagged and produced Usain Bolt, it wasn't God creating a superhuman; it was science. Sometimes Usain Bolt pops out, and other times, the wires get crossed, and tragedy happens. Nothing is dictating your life. Whether it's casual or serious, a god isn't playing chess with a football game or standing in the hospital with a wand. If you think something is helping you kick a field goal, then your god is confused about what it needs to have a hand in. Likewise, if you think it's dabbing your child with a magic stick and giving it certain talents, remember the babies who were born different. They say faith is epitomized in these moments, and that's exactly what religion does—it forms a scare tactic that has you forgiving a mythical being so you're not on its bad side.

5. Belief is different than religion. Belief is strength in self, and religion is dependence on a god. Belief is waking up in the morning and thinking you're real. It's seeing the stars and trusting your eyes. It's hearing music and thinking reality is paradise. It's harder than putting life in the hands of religion; it's keeping your gut, holding your stomach, taking a breath. If someone asks, "Do you believe?" learn to respond, "In me."

   You might think religion teaches these ideas, but it's different. Everything is rooted in hypocrisy, confusion, and conversion. It's mythical and cultlike, and it is purpose driven to make you a follower. What I'm expressing is rooted in reality and trusting the person you are. You're the only one who can do anything with your life, so why follow something besides you? Self-belief is liberation through truth, and religion is suppression through fantasy. You drive your life, period—just like a kid telling their parents, "I got it." Same thing.

Can God help? Can it help attack your dreams? If believing in one does something for you, know what you're trusting. If you want to talk to a god and convince yourself it's walking with you, go for it. If it gives you confidence and eases your anxiety, then whatever works for you. If things go bad, though—and they will—wouldn't it be easier to know whose fault it was? If you believe in yourself from the start, there's no issue.

My entire mantra is self-belief. Don't waste time on things you don't know to be true or fully understand. The toughest thing for us to accept is being free, so we find comfort in religion. We're scared of freedom because of the responsibility it brings, yet freedom and religion are both based in fear. We fear the god we create, just as much as we fear the freedom that exists in its absence. The difference is that we'd rather be dependent on a god than reliant on ourselves.

Make sure your trust starts and ends with you. You're the only one capable of running toward or away from your dreams, fixing things, and adjusting your actions. Consider taking responsibility and driving your life independently. There's less to worry about, less to depend on, and more to gain. You're the solution to your own life. It might put pressure on you, but it's on nobody else. If you want a life you desire, or you want to live your talent, learn to believe in yourself and let everything else go. When you give credit to a god, you allow it to take the credit. It's easy to toss everything in the hands of religion, but that's exactly what a cop-out is.

Remember, belief is strength in self, faith is strength in action, and the combination is called courage. All is done by you.

CHAPTER 3

Do I Need to Increase My Work Ethic?

Probably. I'm not talking about stereotypical hard work, though. What I'm talking about is learning to work hard and smart. You need both.

An easy visual is this: In basketball, there are two ways to improve—develop your skills or study the game. Doing one will make you better; doing both will make you great. The former is working hard, and the latter is working smart.

Take shooting, for example. If you want a better shot, you practice. If you want to score, you study the game. You analyze everything beyond shooting:

researching your opponent, understanding theory, principles of play, data, and so forth. Shooting is a fraction of what it takes to score, and understanding the sport's depth makes you capable.

Basketball, like anything, requires committing to the entire craft. If you work hard at shooting without working *smart* and studying the game, you'll get half the results. Hard work is the repetition of skills, and studying the game implements them effectively. The two together separate amateurs from the professionals. If you want to be great at whatever dream you're chasing, it requires all of you. The practical side must overlap with the academic side. It doesn't matter if it's a sport or anything else; anybody who ever achieved anything had both.

I'll tell you a story. I met an instructor at a soccer coaching course. He went around the room asking what everyone hoped to gain.

He came to me, and I said, "More than I've learned on my own."

"What do you mean?" he said.

I replied, "I wrote a book called *The Opposition Scouting Portfolio*. I studied over one hundred matches and wrote scouting reports on all them. I chose nine games and compiled them into a book. It addresses the heart of soccer, which are tactics, theory, and everything in between. I value studying more than being taught, so I'm hoping to gain more than I've learned on my own."

He sipped his Starbucks.

This is an example of working smart. Once you're willing to study (the details of basketball, the tactics and theories of soccer, the intricacies of woodworking—anything), then you can hit the repetition of developing what you've learned, doing it over and over until you're good.

Nobody is born great, and talent is either developed or lost. Every arena has nuances that make you proficient, and your willingness to study gets you there. In this context, being in a course is one thing, but what you do independently represents your will and how much you want something. *The Opposition Scouting Portfolio* was a personal commitment, and no number of "coaching courses" could replace it. It taught me more than I could imagine and challenged me in ways I never dreamed. It enlightened me as to where I could improve on the practical side of coaching and scouting and helped me understand soccer holistically.

The idea isn't that you have to study something completely before doing it, but to recognize that they correspond. The two go hand in hand, and neither exists without the other. I was coaching and scouting while writing (I had been for years), and the project enhanced what I was practicing. It impacted everything, from my coaching style to player analysis and opposition scouting. I was watching and reading everything I could get my hands on: film for the game I was analyzing, literature on tactics and theory, history on coaching styles, and so on. The trickle down was extensive, and my commitment separated me. I used it as a vehicle to connect with some of American soccer's most important people (general managers, head coaches, and so forth), and it gave them a reason to engage with me. All this together is the academic side of soccer.

The same goes for anything. Whatever the dream may be that you're chasing, working hard and working smart need each other. "Studying" doesn't mean you have to write a book or take a class, but it equals action. It doesn't matter how you embrace it, as long as you do it—and do it better than others.

Most everyone's commitment is one-dimensional. If you pair working hard and smart, you'll gain an advantage. One can't be favored over the other if you seek excellence. I said earlier that "doing one will make you better; doing both will make you great." Each is singular if you desire partial results but collective if you want to be complete. In the end, you'll develop true confidence because what you gain will be obvious, and what others lack will be apparent.

The one thing all the greats of any profession have in common is that they sweat alone and study when nobody's watching. They combine the two and hang their hat on both. Do the same, and you'll fly.

CHAPTER 4

How Do I Make It Through the Grind?

Tough question, simple fix.

What is the grind? The grind is a major obstacle but minor hurdle. It's cynicism, drama, and truth in one. It's wanting something so bad you'd die for it, yet you never do. It's being the only one who believes in your dream, while nobody believes in you. It's taking two steps forward to go one back, and letting the struggle become your shadow.

You have to peel it back and own it. You have to love it or hate it; either works. You have to make the middle finger your friend and develop an attitude that drives you forward.

The most important thing is accepting that nothing comes easy. The grind will punch you, but it can't break you. Things might come easy for some, but they're lucky. Lucky people are one in a million, but you don't want to be one in a million because you're lucky; you want to be one in a million because you worked. You started here and finished there.

You have to realize that scars give you a soul, and that setbacks make you. You'll swallow everything, but you can handle it. In the words of Jim Carrey, "You can fail at what you don't want, so you might as well take a chance on doing what you love."

Eventually, you'll peel things back and see change. You'll control your days—your sleep schedule, work schedule, and so forth. You'll master everything it takes to accomplish tasks. They'll be small at first, but you'll see success.

After you build a rhythm of small-scale achievements, you'll discover that making it through is as simple as sticking it out. You'll realize you came for the fight and stayed for the war. You'll take pride in your resolve because you're no longer fragile. You'll flip your mindset, stay positive, and understand that between you and the grind, you're the one who's real.

In the end, the grind is everything you hate but nothing you can't love. Think about giving yourself weekly themes, such as "hard work, focus, positive attitude" or "Don't get too up or too down." They'll help you grow, stay confident, and see change. Everything starts and ends with you. You're the only one who can beat the grind, and you're the only one that can lose to it. The bottom line is you deserve nothing, and earn everything. It's tough when you're in it, but there's much to gain; all the clichés of learning about yourself are true. You'll iron out what it takes to reach your dream and realize that getting to know yourself doesn't revolve around a reflection in a mirror. Ultimately, you'll push forward if you want it.

Remember two things:

1. Give your dream the attention, not the grind.

2. Strength and determination are tested, not given.

If you live these ideas, they'll push you. There has to be something you commit to that isn't just "the grind." If your focus is that, it'll consume you. If you blow it up, the grind will inflate; that's a fact. It has to be broken down into key concepts you think will help. For me, those work. I still have them taped to my bathroom mirror. You might consider the same—put it on your car steering wheel or next to your coffee maker; somewhere that's part of your routine. You have to understand that what you'll lean on most in the grind isn't other people, but what you believe.

Like I said about weekly themes, having core ideas is the same, and they coincide. Determine a couple of philosophies (perhaps the ones above) that you never take down from your bathroom mirror, and then add a theme every week that's something different. Keep it simple, but rotate it. It's easy to stray, but the rotation will help you build character successfully. It makes it achievable because it's incremental. Your beliefs make you worthy of chasing a dream in the first place, so practice them daily and live up to it. The grind is nothing scary, and little things focus the big picture.

Remember that everyone knows it's tough, but not everyone thinks it's doable. Start small, and wade through.

CHAPTER 5

Can I Be Happy while Grinding?

You might not. At least, you might not be the happiest version of yourself.

I recall being in it; I was day to day, up all night thinking, writing, working. I was tired twenty-four seven. At one point, I had a job where I had to arrive at 7:00 a.m. Nobody there knew or cared, but it's the price you pay if you want something. I remember coming home and sleeping immediately; I'd fall on my bed like a weight dropping in a gym. I'd get up at 7:00 or 8:00 p.m., eat dinner and then work. I'd go to sleep at 2:00 a.m., then get up at 6:30 a.m. I felt like I was screaming at the bottom of the ocean and nobody could hear. Your dream isn't anyone else's, so it doesn't matter. How stressed, upset, and worried you are is only known to you. You have to accept that what you're working toward will define you later, but what defines you now is everything you wish didn't. You have to stand in that light, and not run.

Here's how you stay happy: make sure optimism is the strongest thing about you. Make sure you're in the grind for the right reason, and you want your dream more than you want to breath. The "right reason" is being positive your goal isn't anyone else's. You're not doing it for someone living vicariously through you, or because somebody thinks it's best. The latter can be positive (a form of support, belief, and so forth), but it must be driven by you. Ownership is the base of happiness, and it carries you when the road winds. It increases your tenacity and helps you dig when times are tough. If the dream isn't yours, you won't fight for it.

Never let go of your self-respect. It's your armor and is so important. If people are judging you, ignore it. As long as you're not judging yourself, you're okay.

Learn to value your family and friends because they'll help if they're real. Keep in mind, though, human interaction is based on skepticism. You smile because you don't trust the person you're talking to, and you don't smile for the same reason. We're really dogs on the inside, sniffing out each other's bullshit. Make sure the family and friends you keep are genuine and want success for you. Sniff it out. The love you receive will always equal the love you give. You get love because people have been loved by you, and naturally, they reciprocate. It isn't karma; it's human nature. This is the case for most people in your grind, but your family and friends should be the opposite. They can be a source of happiness if they sincerely believe in you and want nothing from you. Keep them close if they're real; let them go if they're fake.

Most importantly, don't get sidetracked with things that don't contribute to your goals. Lots of people chase a dream but concern themselves with petty moments that waste their time. I've done it, and here's an example:

I was checking out at a grocery store and heard a man saying things I didn't like.

He said, "I don't understand gays."

I looked up.

He said again to the cashier, "I don't understand gays."

The cashier looked at him.

He continued, "I saw two guys over there. It's not natural."

I spoke. "Put in your card."

He replied, "What?"

I said, "Check out, buddy. It's not about being natural, it's about being genuine. Love is love, can you go?"

He replied, "I'm not talking to you."

"Well, I'm talking to you," I said.

He shook his head and left. I checked out and left.

It's easy to get wrapped up in the absurdity of our world, and it can slow you down. The biggest distractions can come from the smallest moments, and I wanted to slap this guy. Staying focused is a large part of how you remain upbeat in a grind, and if you're angry, you're undisciplined. Focus doesn't discriminate against the size of a distraction, and anything that puts you off course is a diversion.

These moments are irrelevant for a reason. The issue might be significant, but whom you're engaging with isn't. There are two types of people here: those who are smart and know how easy it is, and those who are dumb and don't know how hard it is. If you're engaged with the latter, walk away. The bottom line is that when things upset you, make sure they're related to your dream. If not, let them go. Petty moments surround you, but so does your dream. The question is, Which do you like more?

Staying happy is a commitment to focus. You might not be cheerful, but the more you concern yourself with what matters, the easier it is to be pleasant. If you're irritable, you're distracted, so emphasize what's important, and stay as close to happy as you can. In echoing chapter 4, keep the attention on your dream.

CHAPTER 6

Can I Find Love while Pursuing a Dream?

Sure, but understand the following:

1. If you're single, it's because you haven't found your person, not because you don't have one. Even the bravest of loners have someone they'll connect with, but things happen at various times, and paths cross differently for different people. Everything is timing, and timing is happenstance. Some may never find their person, but it doesn't mean they don't exist.

2. If you're grinding, and spending more time attacking a dream than looking for love, it doesn't mean you won't get it. If you go searching, everything you find will seem real because you want it to be. There's a difference between being open and opening your eyes. A lot of things are seemingly real but definitively fake. Learn to be open without being desperate, and recognize the difference between loving someone and fearing the emotion might pass you by.

3. Know what love is for you. If you settle while working toward a dream because you're scared you might not find it, you'll get a "settled" relationship. For me, love is feeling disarmed. It's not only about your best friend but your favorite person. You feel the difference between gravity and jumping out of a plane; you're grounded but no longer falling. You're no longer in the stands but in the game. Whatever dreamy words you use, you're always better with someone who's love for you is genuine. You can define it poetically or practically, but describing it interlocks

it with your dream. Your goals will exhaust you, so figuring out how love contributes is vital. It should aid your direction, not veer you. It should propel you forward, not pin you down. It should believe in you, not discourage you. If you settle for love that isn't right, your dream takes a back seat.

4. Be honest, and put authenticity over possibility. A story:

   I met a woman at a book store, and we connected over poetry. I told her I was reading one poem a night in a book called *Leaves of Grass*, by Walt Whitman, and "it was about all I could take." She laughed and understood. We both had an appreciation for poetry but also an odd distaste. We found it mesmerizing but ridiculous. We talked further over coffee and connected about life being lived with your "head up," not your "nose down," yet we were just in

> a bookstore. It was sincere, and we fit each other. We talked about goals and life, and the important things to me were important to her. We were straight and knew where we were in life. The dreams we had, we laid out. You might think its quick, but we saw it as direct. We were candid.

People put each other on pedestals, and hesitate to be themselves. There's an idea of your perfect partner, and regardless of whether you meet randomly or not, people don't project their true selves out of fear of scaring someone off. It's the oldest advice in the book, but be yourself. There's no reason to say you're a devoted fan of Walt Whitman when you've read five poems, for example. Be honest from the start. Whether the discussion is humorous or serious, if they're with you, you'll know. Your dream is important and should never hide. Whether you're talking poetry or ambition, it's all part of who you are and where you're going. If you put honesty over possibility, you'll get something real. It might not be what you want, but it'll be true. You'll come together, or part ways, but you'll move forward because you were genuine.

Love is trust, and trust is two things: kept or broken. If you fake who you are out of fear someone won't appreciate you, you'll lose trust and eventually love. The one guarantee you have in the grind is the possibility of your dream, so be honest. You can find love while pursuing your goals, but know how they blend and what you want. If you're uncertain, things will fade.

In the end, love will always be like the wind in that it's something you feel, but you don't feel a thing until someone knows you. Remember that you're nobody's half love, and your dream is your first. They can join it and become one, or you let them go. If you're truly grinding, this is important. If they don't run, you've found something worth keeping, and your dream will get easier. The points in this chapter mirror each other but boil down to a single truth: if you're pursuing a goal and hoping to find love in the process, don't carry yourself like a game, and nobody will play you. Be open without being desperate, and put honesty over everything. Your goals and personality define you, so let them shine.

CHAPTER 7

Should I Prioritize Money?

NO.

When it comes to attaining your dream, money should be a result, not a pursuit. There's nothing more important than priorities, and financial belief is one of them. If they're off, your dream is off. Focus on your goal, and let money be a byproduct.

If you think you don't have a dream but just ambition for money, you're unclear what you want. You're after respect, power, influence, clout, security, and so forth. These are dreams too. You're seeking something deeper, but haven't stepped back enough to see it. Find another way to achieve those, and let money come. Nothing empties you like the superficial, and you'll do it to yourself. Ambition rooted in money is destructive. Pinpoint what you truly want, and it'll be sincere. Even if it's power, don't equate it to money, and you'll stand a chance at doing something positive when you get it.

When you chase what doesn't matter, you lose sight of what does. Everyone's situation is different, but there's a common truth to getting your priorities straight. Just because you come from the gutter, it doesn't mean you develop a mindset of financial greed, and just because you're born into privilege, it doesn't mean you get one either. We're all products of our environments but also our personalities. Plenty of folks from both places turn out to be givers, philanthropists, and logical thinkers when it comes to money and the amount they need. No matter where you come from, get your priorities straight. There's no excuse for chasing money. Go after a dream of doing good work and achieving a position that allows you to influence others, give back, and change the world for the better. Chasing money will bury you, and it is preventable.

Look at the endgame. A dream should make you happy. If you're smart, you'll continue without chasing money and appreciate making a living doing what you love. If not, you'll muddle it with the superficial. Satisfaction is often misconstrued. If your dream provides income, it's a mistake to think more money is the next step. It never is. The next step is personal growth; being influential, transcendent, and the best at what you do matters. The level at which you continue impacting the world shows how satisfied you are, not how much money you're making. The latter shows how lost you are. You're not confused if you don't prioritize money, but you are clear on which direction is forward. If you emphasize what's important, you'll keep your heart in it, and more money will come.

When pursuing a dream, think, "Am I masking things? Do I want my dream or do I want money? Can I keep my goals at the center?" If you don't chase money, you'll control your dream. If not, money controls you. If you achieve what you want but lose yourself in the process, you'll have nothing. Maybe you think chasing money won't diminish things, but it will. Mimicking who you were before it dominated your goals is impossible. You get one chance to keep your soul. If you sell it, it leaves.

There's nothing wrong with money, as long as you're grounded on how to achieve it. Go after your dream, and let it come. If you chase it, you'll lose every direction you ever had. I said this in chapter 1: "What you want is what you need, and what you need is what you want." This refers to a dream based in passion, not a quest centered on money. There's a difference between being big and being rich. I want you to be known and for your dream to manifest and be great, but accomplish it without prioritizing the superficial. If you're lucky enough to find what wakes you up in life, don't let something shallow overtake it. I'd rather you be famous with a voice than rich with a black card. Be the best, and money will come.

CHAPTER 8

What Is Success?

Happiness: Whatever your journey, this is the destination.

Where people struggle is lacking conviction. It's the most important prerequisite, and without it, success is impossible. If you measure yourself against others and don't believe in what you're doing, you'll get a delusional idea of achievement.

I remember driving with my best friend in high school, listening to "Heart of the City," by Jay-Z. There's a lyric about what others eat not making you shit. It's funny, but it might as well be Plato.

Not caring what others think is tough, but doable. Your life goes through waves, ups and downs, ages, periods, relationships, and moments, and having conviction is tough. If people say they liked the "old you," it's always because your conviction was strong, and somewhere along the line you lost it. They secretly miss attaching to you. People find it impossible to develop conviction on their own, so they cling to someone who has it and think they're part of its energy. Conviction isn't that easy. It might be inspiring, but it doesn't hand itself over. You have to go get it.

Success is happiness, and happiness starts with conviction. I could give you a redundant speech about working a job you hate and not doing what you love, but why? It's the most overtold idea in history, and there's a thousand self-help books that will hold your hand around the same thing. It's not about pumping you up. It's about asking if you truly believe in happiness. It's about being honest and questioning whether you're a believer in its certainty. It's easy to believe in unhappiness, but what about the opposite?

Think of it like this: you're sitting in an office doing something you hate. It's four o'clock, and bam—in that moment, you know unhappiness is real. Why? Because it's smacking you in the face. The issue is that happiness, unlike its ugly counterpart, doesn't hit you in the face. It's earned, and is something you reach out for (like conviction). Unhappiness is glaring, and happiness is mysterious. You second-guess the latter because it doesn't hit you. You say things like, "Is it actually better?" You're doubtful, and you hesitate to believe.

Happiness and conviction work together. They're one and the same, and neither is given. You have to believe in yourself and what you want and think that in the end, it equals happiness. Whether you're purpose driven with a need to influence, or moderate without a care, happiness will always determine the size of your life. It's the one eternal craving we share, and is more desirable than money and power combined. Nothing else defines success. You're unsuccessful if you're unhappy, and you're unhappy without conviction. It is as simple as that.

CHAPTER 9

Am I Talented?

Why wouldn't you be? Know the following:

1. As I said earlier, talent is either developed or lost; it will not carry you on its own. You have to believe it and live every day like you have something to prove. There's a common quote: "Hard work beats talent when talent doesn't work hard." If you're talented but don't work like you're starving, your dream is impossible. Before wondering if you have talent, wonder if you have desire.

2. If you're not great at the first thing you try, it doesn't mean you're not talented at something else. If you're beating your head against a wall, either don't stop until you break it, or find another one. Either accept it may take a lifetime to be good at that one thing, or stop and explore something else. The choice is yours.

3. Regardless of where you come from, everyone is talented. If you start at a disadvantage, it may take longer, but you'll discover what you're good at. Look at it like this: disadvantages are like driving a car through a congested city. If you zoom out and see things from the air, it's easy to view routes and ways to go. The underprivileged are on the ground, and the privileged are in the air. When people wonder why you don't take certain avenues to achieve success, they're always up high.

Don't concern yourself with their judgment, and focus on how the ground can make you great. All the wrong turns or bad roads you go down make you better. Maybe you reroute, maybe not, but being on the ground clarifies things in ways people in the air will never know.

Remember this: the difference between you and people in the air is that you discover a soul. Within your struggle, you have to reach down and see if you have one. It's called soul searching. It gives you an appreciation for your goals and makes you smarter, stronger, and more resilient. You'll value what you achieve because you earned it. You'll discover you had the stomach to push through hardship. You'll go through doubt and learn what guts are. You'll be forced to find answers, because life asked you questions: "Do I still want this?" "How far am I willing to go?" It'll make you seesaw, but the back and forth will help you balance. It'll give you a fighting spirit and make you worth believing. What you eventually achieve, the world will accept because you went through the wringer and survived. Most importantly, being on the ground will teach you to live with strength instead of coping with weakness.

Starting on the ground will always be better than the air. Remember that people up high are phony and entitled, and you're genuine and justified. There's nothing sweet about having it easy, and though the grind is tough when you're in it, your success will be true when you get it. People in the air can't say that. Learn to grow from the ground, and be fiercer than the people looking down on you.

Ultimately, talent is everywhere and in everyone. The toughest thing isn't others questioning you, but you not believing in yourself. You have to see talent as the most insignificant part of achievement and your struggle like an advantage. If you never stop working, thinking, and pounding the pavement, good things happen. It might be an opportunity, it could be an idea, but it'll come from your fight. Nothing is easy, and you need more than talent.

CHAPTER 10

What's It All About?

Believing in yourself and attacking your dream is about one thing, and that's happiness. You can have what you want.

When you fail, don't quit. Look up, forward, and never behind. Maybe you fail again, maybe not, but keep going. Remember that true happiness doesn't come from throwing in the towel. The road is never clear, but your objective stays the same. You might try new things, and go to new places, but keep your eye on the ball, and your dream in focus. If you're sincere, you'll succeed. Be the person who thinks taking a dare in "truth or dare" is a cop-out.

The toughest thing for a lot of people with a dream is that, in some form, you're antiestablishment. Popularity doesn't echo with you, but merit does. You don't buy into suck-ups, and you know if you join them, you become one. Though you're an outcast in the beginning, it's precisely why you'll succeed.

Remember that living your dream inspires others to do the same. Whatever your ceiling is, know it's a lie. Your life and potential are never limited, and your ceiling is an illusion. You control what you want, how far you go, and how deep your fear runs. Happiness and your dream will always be around the corner, and are never out of reach. You can take your time or go fast; there are no rules.

Be confident in everything you do, and live with conviction. Care what nobody thinks. Confidence is medicine and also your shining light. If happiness is the finish line, start here.

Accept that adversity makes you. Some paths are longer than others, but if you're honest and producing the best work, happiness will come. Learn to see the poetry in the struggle and romance in the hardship. It's important for when you finally succeed. You'll look back at where you were and forward to where you're going. When everyone around you is crumbling, be the one who endures. The more you fight and break down walls, the stronger you are, and the closer your dream gets. Fragility might define you in the beginning, but durability represents you in the end.

If I leave you with one thing, it's this: the world might not see your ability, but I do. I'm the odd gift of being the talent you spot but the one who spots talent. I see you, but I want you to see yourself. The greatest problem you'll face isn't that you aren't big-time, but rather that people don't care you're small. What I care about is the unknown talent nobody sees. I want the world to care and for you to be big. I think everyone can be brilliant. Just because you aren't Einstein, it doesn't mean you're not you.

With that said, remember that if you look for the lie in someone's dream, you'll find it in a second, but look for the truth, and you'll spend all day. It's easy to spot someone who isn't serious, but you can be the opposite. If you're willing to work, you can achieve anything. Your talent is there, but how much you want something makes it true. If you want it, work for it.

Always know that your life doesn't hang in the balance if your dream is at the center. Keep it in front of you, stay strong, and never stop.

Good luck.

The End

About the Author

Rob Fisher is a soccer scout and writer. Born and raised in North Carolina, he graduated from Guilford College and went on to serve three years in the US Peace Corps. Posted in Eswatini, he used soccer as an instrument to teach about HIV/AIDS and worked at the youth and professional level. He coached a rural high school to two conference titles, one regional championship, and a national semifinal. Shortly after, he began scouting professionally in the United States and released his first eBook, *RF Volume I: The Opposition Scouting Portfolio.* He's currently starting a nonprofit that discovers players in marginalized talent territories, and he was inspired by his time abroad.

His writing is brave, original, and nonconforming. He believes in equal opportunity and doing what you love.

www.meetrobfisher.com

Instagram: @rfisher451

CPSIA information can be obtained
at www.ICGtesting.com
Printed in the USA
LVHW022151120523
746813LV00010B/679

Yes, There Are Stupid Questions is an insurgent in the self-help genre. Concise enough to hold your attention and interesting enough to inspire you it answers subconscious questions people ask when attacking a dream.

In a time when verbosity prevails and the mundane is accepted it stands in opposition by offering something unique and to the point. Eliminating monotonous advice and meaningless filler pages it frames things to help you think, reflect, and move forward differently.

Complete with quotable tidbits and new guidance it's nothing you'll expect but everything you'll need. You'll appreciate the balance between depth and practicality and the blend of candor and sarcasm.

Topics include:

Religion

Love

Money

Happiness

Made in Charleston, SC
www.PalmettoPublishingGroup.com